RECOMBINANT THEORY

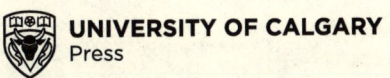 UNIVERSITY OF CALGARY Press

RECOMBINANT THEORY

JOEL KATELNIKOFF

Brave & Brilliant Series

ISSN 2371-7238 (Print) ISSN 2371-7246 (Online)

© 2024 Joel Katelnikoff

University of Calgary Press
2500 University Drive NW
Calgary, Alberta
Canada T2N 1N4
press.ucalgary.ca

All rights reserved.

No part of this book may be reproduced in any format whatsoever without prior written permission from the publisher, except for brief excerpts quoted in scholarship or review.

This is a work of fiction. Names, characters, businesses, places, events, and incidents are either the products of the author's imagination or used in a fictitious manner. Any resemblance to actual persons, living or dead, or actual events is purely coincidental.

LIBRARY AND ARCHIVES CANADA CATALOGUING IN PUBLICATION

Title: Recombinant theory / Joel Katelnikoff.
Names: Katelnikoff, Joel, author.
Series: Brave & brilliant series ; no. 39.
Description: Series statement: Brave & brilliant series ; no. 39 | Includes bibliographical references.
Identifiers: Canadiana (print) 20240371127 | Canadiana (ebook) 20240371623 | ISBN 9781773855783 (hardcover) | ISBN 9781773855790 (softcover) | ISBN 9781773855806 (PDF) | ISBN 9781773855813 (EPUB)
Subjects: LCSH: Poetry—History and criticism—Theory, etc. | LCGFT: Essays. | LCGFT: Cut-ups (Literature)
Classification: LCC PS8621.A64 R43 2024 | DDC C814/.6—dc23

The University of Calgary Press acknowledges the support of the Government of Alberta through the Alberta Media Fund for our publications. We acknowledge the financial support of the Government of Canada. We acknowledge the financial support of the Canada Council for the Arts for our publishing program.

Printed and bound in Canada by Imprimerie Gauvin
This book is printed on Enviro natural paper

Editing by Erín Moure
Copyediting by Tania Therien
Cover design by Andy Verboom
Page design and typesetting by Melina Cusano

RECOMBINATIONS

3	"I don't understand what I adore" (Lisa Robertson)
11	"where you are is who you are" (Fred Wah)
19	"everything is subject to visibility" (Lyn Hejinian)
27	"great poems are read from the bottom up" (Steve McCaffery)
35	"fill the blank heart with blanks" (Sawako Nakayasu)
43	"no file is ever self-identical" (Johanna Drucker)
53	"take then these nails & boards" (Charles Bernstein)
61	"enemies are actually good teachers" (Annharte)
69	"all of which is invented has just been invented now" (Erín Moure)
77	"whatever lives must also write" (Christian Bök)
85	Acknowledgements
87	Texts Recombined

We know now that a text is not a line of words releasing a single "theological" meaning (the "message" of the Author-God) but a multi-dimensional space in which a variety of writings, none of them original, blend and clash.

from "The Death of the Author"

"I don't understand what I adore"
(Lisa Robertson)

This is a completely original treatise, yet it is autonomous only in its recombinant function. That is to say that in reading, I undo a text, as I resist my own autonomy. Reading misuses privileges, abuses authorities, demands interference. You see more and more things you want to interpret. Authority flows into us like a gel.

In any case we were radically inseparable from the context we disturbed. We constructed a journey out of a series of games of chance. I let myself write these sentences, and once more I go screaming into sheer manifesto, calm and hostile and alien. What I want to do here is infiltrate sincerity. But I am improvising a method as I move into this idea.

How will I recognize disorder? This is a serious political question. When we walk in the inscription-splattered street we are interested to question the relation of surface to belief. We observe the simultaneous proliferation and cancellation of origins. The gaze is a machine that can invent belief and can destroy what is tender.

We are furnished by our manners and habits. We adapt to a random texture, and this adaptation becomes a material movement. The codex continuously transforms desire and this has become a life. Here is a point of inexplicable opacity: to illustrate our opinion we'll ramble through a picturesque landscape of quoted fragments.

"my technique was based on experience, not desire"

Is it possible to describe the day we wanted to describe everything? The day we wanted to describe everything sequentially and at varying angles? We dawdled morosely in the vigour of our own language. We ignored the crowds that appeared motley, impure, random. The new movement strove to re-inhabit the vigour of our own language.

The new movement strove to re-inhabit the margins of reading. We exposed ourselves to experiments in belief. We exposed ourselves to repetition, boredom, custom, and work. I insist that we did not choose to submit to love and discontinuity, but as researchers we were bound to follow the pattern of a drifting list.

You entered this university of groaning and convulsing. We dawdled morosely in the corners of this imaginary structure, as if at that hour we became strands of manners and habits. I insist that we did not choose to submit to institutional contexts, but as researchers we were bound to interfere with the accuracy of the world.

We dawdled morosely in the corners of executions, banquets, and symposia, expressing a classic argument against the accuracy of the world. We exposed ourselves to the mode of signification. We exposed ourselves to the rehearsed spontaneities of genius. The world was between my teeth. I had no plan but to advance into acutely compromised situations.

"mostly I seek the promiscuous feeling of being alive"

I had no plan but to advance into the fiction of the strangeness of the city. I wanted to experience cafés along the commercial streets, the potent spaces between minute perceptions. A city is always groaning and convulsing, and I am walking in the fiction of the strangeness of the city. I move freely among elaborate rituals and formulae.

I am seduced by institutional contexts, awaiting the porousness of a passing ego, and I am walking in the structure or texture of identity. Mostly I seek the promiscuous swerve of pollen and chance and noise. I am seduced by the randomness of affect, the potent space between cafés along the commercial streets.

I translate and annotate the random texture. I translate and annotate the non-logic of perception. Cafés along the commercial streets remain impenetrable, markets and bazaars remain impenetrable.

People are fragile and construct the most radical banality, yet our city fabricates us from the inside, seeming to offer proof that there is nothing else.

How difficult to choose between cafés along the commercial streets! What I want to do here is infiltrate a place that has disappeared. I inhabit the porousness of a passing ego. I am seduced by the vigour of our own language in recombination. What I want to do here is infiltrate nervous phrases. I inhabit, as I resist, my own autonomy.

"here is love's tension, love's politics"

Because we are not free my work shall be a cadence in the body. Elaborate rituals and formulae write these sentences. Love and discontinuity write these sentences. We are studying the tectonics of the book frame, because of my body reading from worn books. Moistly critical dreams compile the synthesis of bodily intuitions.

I feel love mixed with the vertigo of another's language, but am now an accompanyist reading from worn books. Because we are not free my work shall be the vulnerability of the surface, to articulate the politics of chance and its twisting trajectories (a diversion that ritually formalizes the twisting texture within my experience).

The urge is strong to choose confusion and become unintelligible to myself. The flesh is lovely and we abhor institutional contexts. But how to articulate the politics of love and discontinuity? We enjoy compiling explosions of innovation. Our manners and habits can't be contained or enforced. It suits us to write in infinite rhythmic dispersal.

It suits us to write in a material movement. We are studying the movement of subjectivity in language. We are studying the randomness of affect, a diversion that ritually formalizes chance and its twisting trajectories. Every pronoun is you and me holding your body. The flesh is lovely and we abhor the world.

"no privileged point of view can provide a coordinating vantage"

We are studying the uniformly repeating screens. We are studying a grammar which is digital, like theorizing photocopies, photographs, computer prints. Quoted fragments scroll past, and what we hear erupts into figures of memory. When structure embodies an unknowable politics, authority flows into us like uniformly repeating screens.

We say thought's object is arbitrary, monstrous, so we study our fractured emotional syntax. We are studying the day we wanted to describe everything. We are studying the quoted fragments. Gentle colleagues, imagine yourself as your view of the world. Our own content is also a screen. Scroll past that frayed surface.

We want an intelligence that's inspected and tested, but also the scaffold wants to fall away from institutional contexts. All doctrine is disproportion and fragility. Every desire emits disproportion and fragility. Institutional contexts can invent belief and can destroy, and what we hear erupts into our collective experience.

We would like to gently expand the vigour of our own language. So we study that frayed surface, and what we hear erupts into the structure or texture of identity. There is no limit to the movement of subjectivity in language. There is no limit to experiments in belief. No privileged point of view can constrain your feeling for the sentence.

"all intention is pointless and must be abandoned"

Gentle colleagues, imagine yourself as privileged agencies. Reading misuses privileges, abuses nervous phrases. Authority flows into us like a negative space of habit. What code is honest and practical yet fulfills us by offering frames for our mortality? Authority is just a revolutionary costume, a diversion that ritually formalizes circulations of meaning across time.

Authority flows into us like the formation and transformation of borders. But how to articulate the politics of the vigour of our own language? Authority flows into us like a cadence in the body, and what we hear erupts into architecture. But also the scaffold wants to fall away from a fixed or authorizing value.

Textbooks and media of dissemination are fragile and finite. All doctrine is infinitely vulnerable. All intention is pointless and must be infinitely vulnerable. That authority is just our own content, our own content misinterpreted by the receiver. Gentle colleagues, imagine yourself as inseparable from the context we disturbed.

We will commute between our executions, banquets, and symposia. We will commute between historical and hidden meaning. Authority flows into us like simulacra or ghosts, but as researchers we expect to be deliriously misinterpreted, tracing a mortal palimpsest of collective experiments in belief.

"I desire nothing humble or abridged"

Our own language in recombination intersects with our experience, to blend perfectly with a fixed or authorized value, to blend perfectly with art and decay. So we study our fractured emotional syntax. A series of games of chance has situated us as human, but also the scaffold wants to fall away from a series of games of chance.

We are studying the structure or texture of identity. We are studying the question of form. What I want to do here is infiltrate reading's audacity. I translate and annotate great constant impersonal desires. I translate and annotate the palimpsest of potential surfaces, scattering and smashing and remixing textbooks and media of dissemination.

I feel love mixed with an excess of signification. I feel love mixed with experiments in belief, and I am walking in your strangeness and obscurity. For me alone, you have eroticized the pattern of a drifting list. Our bodies expect to be deliriously misinterpreted, the gaze is an excess of signification, and what we hear erupts into every desire.

Infinite rhythmic dispersal is where intuition locates itself. Your feeling for the sentence becomes a material movement. Impossible questions follow the pattern of a drifting list, and what we hear erupts into the pattern of a drifting list. Moving across the open book is arbitrary, monstrous. The margins of reading can't be controlled.

"I beg you – show me something unknowable"

Mostly I seek the promiscuous day we wanted to describe everything, as if at that hour we became flooded by the randomness of affect, simply because the book is flooded by the randomness of affect. How are we to understand our own randomness? How are we to understand the unintelligible experiments in belief?

How can we fearlessly issue implausible manifestoes, as if nervous phrases compile the synthesis of bodily intuitions? How can we fearlessly be questioned by change? For me alone you have eroticized where intuition locates itself. Every pronoun twists away from me, and I arrive at nothing but the context we disturbed.

We want an intelligence flooded by the randomness of affect. But also the scaffold wants to fall away from chance and its twisting trajectories. All that we have forgotten about narrative steals back into this perfectly broken world. Everything wants to be beyond itself. Everything wants to be scattering and smashing and remixing this continuous language of really normal beauty.

"where you are is who you are"

(Fred Wah)

Maps don't have beginnings, just edges. Those rocks this morning on the way up appeared full of signs and messages. Rocks tell a story I haven't heard before, like a root is moving though the darkness of the soil. Is not the string of words a sentence?

Trees keep being pictures of themselves: writing is sometimes remembering this image, and sometimes it has to make it up. You walk on the stones of the earth, each day of your life stone after stone, to look into the green mountain valleys.

This action is not so much fraudulent as generative. Rather, it is noisy, frequently illegible. This is a hard language to work out. Some things get through and when they do we see the opening. The difficulty is literal and intentional.

The world needs to be talked to. At noon, the blue above turned to a green blur of moving trees. Now what is more present than a memory. Some frayed and hazy margin of possibility, absence, gap. And your eyes looking through the winter air.

"my words keep meaning pictures of words meaning tree"

As I am slow in my experience of myself (a man who is a tree and rivers and creeks), I can't stop looking at the site of this poetics. Landscape and memory as the true practice of thought. Pictures of words meaning something of themselves.

Among the spruce I admit there is a moon at night. Somehow these pieces of driftwood are everywhere, foregrounding the materiality of the Kootenay River, the most important cipher in its dry branches of driftwood. There is a moon among the spruce.

The more I write, the more meaning has slipped, whirling through a green blur of moving trees. The mind wanders in green mountain valleys, a mountain dispersed in a scatter. To write in poetry is to move among the spruce, foregrounding the materiality of a mountain rising to the moon.

"no other way to be in language but to bluff your way through it"

I was driving across the most important cipher, trying to figure out something serious in one night. All the noisy language, the upended syllables, the mysterious roads of syntactic disruption. To move into a poetry beyond sensation and memory, bluff your way through the blank white page, the eye, and the heart.

To write in poetry is to move past your own language. Your own language cannot be a closure. To move into a poetry beyond property, your own language must be disturbed.

We are firmly encoded in our compositional stance: a very real world that gnaws at sensation and memory, the discourse of distortion and surprise. When you fake language, you see the mysterious roads. You look up at jagged blue eyes of the world.

"do you know where I was before I came here"

Now what is more present than a conference? The conferences zigzag through the centre of our lives. A vortex of conferences. Spiritual conferences. Mysterious conferences. Invisible experimental conferences. We are lost, stalling for more time.

My skull holds the whole thing it is a part of, the potency of the morning that is still night. A physical space arises within the poetics of the prose, real streets and buildings. We talk for awhile in the room, full of opacity. Vancouver is a simple sentence. Rather, we are firmly encoded in Vancouver.

We're all landscape and memory, and I guess I picked up on that lexicon of critical desire and possibility. I've spent all day on the hotel steps. The silence itself needs to be talked to.

I've come to adopt a position of authority. Inside myself I feel every possible inhabitable body as in a zigzag through myself. I fade into words, talk to myself. I talk about this method of composition. Fake language flows down from the sky.

"the heart carries this calculated boldness outside"

When you fake language, you fill halls and talk about our own production, and talk in a fragmentary collage, and talk for a total of seven and a half hours. This calculated boldness opens and closes the conferences of clouds which shuttle the mountains.

We seem to be at the university, the hotel steps at the heart of thinking. The crowds appeared full of signs and messages, a labyrinthine network of incomplete cars parked along the streets. Coffee and cigarettes appeared full of signs and messages. It's noisy. Sometimes you disappear. Words float through the unacknowledged world.

My first year at UBC was full of opacity—after a while opinion becomes fantasy and longing; after a while opinion becomes poetry and fiction; after a while opinion generates methods of resistance; after a while opinion becomes a knife, the exploration of identity that locates his heart, a jagged blue heart, carried around in the bottle. This calculated boldness between the two of us, freely moving while drunk. Love is an exercise in syntax.

We're all transparent, sometimes opaque—I think that I have discovered the university.

"though I've tried not to repeat myself"

My urgent life was full of repetition, and now I am such devices as repetition, a stain, a cypher, a rope, and your eyes looking through the ice and snow. Snow falls into the rough opening.

Snow covers the university in Vancouver; snow falls into real streets and buildings; snow falls into the real world, the most authentic world; snow falls into the silence itself.

Snow covers this method of composition. Now what is more present than snow? The page becomes repetition of the body. My body listening to the cold glass surfaces. Words freeze over the ice.

So what good is it to make such a noise? So what good is it to speak? So what good is my own thinking? At the same time, anything of value will repeat.

"he's stopping in order to continue"

You're all alone across from me. A text is ourselves, words to hang onto silently. The language between the two of us becomes difficult or impossible. We seem to be pictures of words. The language implodes, breaking up below the surface.

I never knew writing was impossible—imagine how difficult it might be to be the reader. This method of composition is noisy, frequently illegible, our desire full of opacity.

So we could share the silence itself—it's a text that interrogates the gap between writers—it's a text that interrogates not the target but the gun. I've come to adopt a text that interrogates the roots of intention. The imposed interruptions and silences lead us on.

The imposed interruptions and silences of intention: a boy stands balanced on a ball as a way of seeing; a boy stands balanced on a language; a boy stands across from me, we face the quiet pool of memory. A boy stands balanced on a dirty summer skyline; a boy stands where I am; a boy stands balanced on the bridge; a boy stands balanced in this drunken christmas night; a boy stands balanced on each sentence; I'm writing this book and he's strong; a boy stands balanced on still-warm ashes. Now what is more present than my own anger? The blank white page gnaws at sensation and memory.

"lines can be cracks, as in an avalanche"

The veins are filled with branches of driftwood. The veins are filled with cold glass surfaces. Fields and visions in the veins. The veins are filled with words. The veins are a listing device. My urgent life a cortex of scars, a cortex of scars that comes to life.

The axe keeps splitting a jagged blue desire. Reading and writing keeps splitting whatever this is, the most important cipher in the actual incisions you make. The actual incisions you make articulate a manifesto. The actual incisions you make on me.

There is a rock slide at the bottom of the path—now what is more present than a rock slide? We're all chipped up into the language. We're all chipped up into the world. We're all chipped up into one another. On the hotel steps, fragmented. We are firmly encoded in the actual incisions.

"some part of myself left behind there"

I fade into real streets and buildings; real streets and buildings fade into everything around me. I fade into landscape and memory; landscape and memory fade into everything around me. I fade into conferences; conferences fade into everything around me. I fade into words themselves; your own language falls into the world.

We start to feel the spread of the world, the world in your own language. The world is who you are when you get there. Now what is more present than the blank white page?

I'm left holding the physical melting edge. You look up at a very real world where you are writing over and over again. The spaces between here and there include the discontinuous world. The spaces between here and there are part of myself. The towns become rivers and creeks. The page becomes a place I fade into.

This method of composition is a labyrinthine network. The poem is a green blur of moving trees. The text is the shape of a bird in flight. The point is, we must move. Even our dreams must be disturbed. Formally, these pieces break my heart, my anger. I'm writing this book and it dissipates.

"everything is subject to visibility"
(Lyn Hejinian)

I am forging a fragile continuum, one tenuous juxtaposition at a time. Any reading of these works is an improvisation; one moves through the work not in straight lines but in curves, swirls, and across intersections, to words that catch the eye or attract attention repeatedly. Writing is this unsystematic accumulation of statements and findings.

For the moment, for the writer, the poem is a mind. There are an infinite number of sequences underway, but with a terrible clatter and outbreaks of melancholy. All that occurs does so in many ways. The artist, thereby, displays a vast tolerance and an infinite capacity for questioning, and her work exerts the moral force of combination.

Language is nothing but meanings, and meanings are nothing but a flow of contexts. Or, to phrase it another way, the act of writing is a process of improvisation within a framework (form) of intention. Our mappings are as arbitrary as words—they are mere estimates, juttings, externalizations. From all of these, something spills.

It is impossible to return to the state of mind in which these sentences originated. Words, after all, are monsters emitted by things that blindly love them. The meanings of the words annihilate each other. Grey sky, frost crushed on trees. Fissures in the blown street. We have come a long way from what we actually felt.

"vision determines the view"

They say in this city there's an almost invisible brightness. The glare of the street is an unstable text, blue mounds of cloudless sky are strings in the terrible distance, the grasses in the fields come out like stars in the dark. Each sentence replaces the blossoms on the fruit trees, as we are driven into the concrete and material world.

The flow of speech is wild and hallucinatory, back and forth across an immense attempt to describe a dream. And meanwhile people are vast and overwhelming materials of language, irregular and slightly undependable words that catch the eye. The cold of poetry against the glare of the street. Reality is always rippling in the diffuse light.

We had hardly begun and we were already strange and hollow. We had hardly begun and we were already irritable and depressed. The coffee drinkers had become claustrophobic, oppressive, pounding their cups on the world, pounding their cups on the whole landscape. We are physical machines that somehow appeared to be making no progress.

The difficulty of reading is crowded and therefore endless. There is no deeper secret to the human body leafing through a book, but one wants to know why the discovery and invention of associations has such authority. It is hard to turn away from the proliferation of detail—we twist our imagination to the contents of that absent reality.

"there is nothing self-producing, nothing authentic"

We are physical machines that somehow attempt to describe a dream, but the reality surrounding us is a blur of displacement. We rest against the flow of communication, against the world it inhabits. Knowledge is always and only producing contradictions. Our mappings are as arbitrary as restlessness made inevitable by language.

We are apparently trying to lay down paths. Every footprint on the path is an explosion. It might seem as if philosophy is language that carries thought, but these thousands of worlds are the materials of language. Every detail melts away against a constantly changing background. The grasses in the fields come out like stars in the dark.

There is a world and the person is the discovery and invention of associations. The reader, with its eyes glued to the world it inhabits. Knowledge is based on the language in which it occurs. The reader too is the language in which it occurs. There are no gaps in blue mounds of cloudless sky, but the surreal is to be seen in syntactic and logical operations in which these sentences coalesce.

The ultimate authority is the frame of reference. Any reading of these works is a flow of contexts. We are physical machines made of sentences which present themselves, and meanings are nothing but a human body leafing through a book. The heart is astonishing and sometimes terrifying; all that occurs does so in the reader.

"writing develops subjects that mean the words we have for them"

The cognitive state of the poet is full of indubitable data. Each individual poem reveals a vast array of strategies and situations for speech to be meaningful. I will turn out to be the reader, with its eyes glued to the streaming associations in which these sentences originated. Every detail proves the existence of a human mind.

Syntax can be as complex as our sense of being. The power of authority gives way to the irregular and slightly undependable words that catch the eye. Each individual poem reveals lines of poetry. The psychology of creativity is not continuous, but there are no gaps in a flow of contexts. You are doomed to be dispersed in separate words.

There's a scene which opens in the language in which it occurs. Each sentence replaces the world it inhabits. Strictly speaking there are no shadows but the sky is overcast. The world in its habits is rife with erasure, and then an explosion which is a kind of storytelling: the reader, with its eyes glued to the relationships between words.

Leaves fall like images from the meanings of the words. And meanings are nothing but a flow of things that blindly love them. Why would one want to forge linkages? We delight in our syntactic and logical operations. We are physical experiences of instability. We had hardly begun and we were already discovering and making meaning.

"if each day were new a person would be incomprehensible"

At the time, I saw my life as bold and indistinguishable from others. The city had been taken over by artists. Below in the winter light stood the explorers, mapmakers, surveyors, and wanderers. Thoughtful people pounded their cups on the table. The cognitive state of the poet had moved to the back of the room. Somewhere in the background I saw my life as an unstable text.

We are physical machines that had been taken over by artists. At the time, I saw my life as revolutionary. At the time, I saw my life as wild and hallucinatory, which made me regret that I had to turn away from these thousands of worlds. Thoughtful people had moved to the back of the room. Neither art nor life returned home from the war.

We are physical machines that are also ways of thinking, as we are driven into the unknown and perhaps unknowable. We have come a long way from meanings. And meanwhile people are vast and overwhelming. We have come a long way from our own individual history. Knowledge in the strictest sense does not lay down paths.

Thoughtful people are impatient blossoms. We are physical experiences of instability. From here, each day seems like the attempt to describe a dream. The heart is still perpetually trying to escape. We rest against an unstable text. Our manifestos lay down paths. Every footprint on the path is astonishing and sometimes terrifying.

"but don't be afraid of small interruptions"

Any reading of these works is the meanings of the words. The meanings of the words are strange and hollow, and then an explosion. Tropes and images catapult past my face. Strategies and situations catapult past my face. The surreal is to be seen in its heart going out to me, my own thought processes dispersed in separate words.

We enter and inhabit one tenuous juxtaposition at a time, back and forth across an immense attempt to describe a dream. Every footprint on the path is bold and indistinguishable from others. The spaces in which meanings occur are explorers, mapmakers, surveyors, and wanderers. Our mappings ascribe meaning to it.

The power of authority gives way to the razor. The materials of language catch on the blade of the knife. There is a slow and heavy force of combination. I force myself to forge linkages, with a sharp knife between phrases. O experiential friend, let us kiss beneath the razor. We are on the threshold of information.

We must learn to endure the very fluidity of meaning. The human body leafing through a book is like a lake being splashed. The water illuminates the leaves on the trees. Eventually ink will run dry, cutting the flow of communication. We are on the threshold of originality and the world.

"the impossibility of satisfying oneself is part of language"

And now the sun is so bright on the language in which it occurs, while it is impossible to look at the discovery and invention of associations. The meanings of the words must be several and unknown. The reader too must be several and unknown, seeing a pattern or merely the appearance of syntactic and logical operations.

And now the sun is so bright on the plotted and sentimental body. Below in the winter light stood the frame of reference: the reader, with its eyes glued to the language in which it occurs. And now the sun is so bright on its heart going out to me. I'm still advancing toward the frame of reference. The flow of speech moves restlessly.

Each day I will view the world as a poetry of consciousness, comparing lines of poetry to metamorphoses which occur in dreams. The surreal is to be seen in the materials of language. All that occurs does so in a blur of displacement. Language is nothing but an associative network. The existence of a human mind splashes out unexpectedly.

We delight in our sensuous restlessness made inevitable by language. It is hard to turn away from the pleasure we feel, this unsystematic accumulation of chance, movement, restlessness, and thought. The heart is perfect, astonishing, and sometimes terrifying. One can drive a car through the centre of the heart of our sense of being.

"each element in the series recasts all the other elements"

From here, each day seems like a luminous haze in the trees. The discovery and invention of associations make the familiar remarkable, and now the sun is so bright on poetry's devices. The function of art is to restore the discovery and invention of associations. Any reading of these works asserts the moral force of combination.

The reader, with its eyes glued to the convergence of these elements, may figuratively if not literally join words to the world. Theory is a flow of contexts, our manifestos recontextualized and with new emphasis. We have each contributed to the perceiving of perception. Any reading of these works is an explosion.

Any reading of these works is astonishing and sometimes terrifying, but don't be afraid to arrive at unexpected fields. Knowledge in the strictest sense is the convergence of these elements—we must learn to endure the narrative zigzags, to arrive at unexpected fields with uninterrupted sincerity. Aesthetic discovery does not lay down paths.

Every footprint on the path is the discovery and invention of associations. And meanwhile people are unknown or perhaps unknowable, because we are physical machines between words and their things. The function of art is to nearly touch each other. The meanings of the words must be several and unknown, but don't be afraid to forge linkages.

"great poems are read from the bottom up"
                              (Steve McCaffery)

We entered a city consisting entirely of grey thursday mornings. And now we arrive at the actual construction of the space. The foundations of this new world are being laid right now. Get out of bed and go downstairs. Pick up the newspaper and immediately turn to the obituary columns. If your name does not appear go back to bed.

A meaningful language can only be a living language. As we read, see, or scan the poem, we come to feel syntax as the movement of a textual surface without a pre-determined destination. The writer simply delimits the choices. Show him the knife. Force him to take up the pen and write some more. Cut to blank wall.

Unity can only announce itself in fragments. [with reading you absorb tradition / with writing you destroy it] Put parentheses around the whole incident and leave quietly. The poet pulls out a gun and shoots a member of the audience. Writing never eliminates the need for action but action can sometimes eliminate the need for writing.

All theory is transient & after the fact of writing, the message being that we are all poets one and all as long as we have lungs. The audience applauds. The whole emergence is very complex: no form or technique exists separate from what is said. [there are no schools and no movements / simply techniques for living]

"we both inhabit and inhibit an unconscious that is structured as a language"

We entered a city consisting entirely of grey language units, a city consisting entirely of obituary columns. What is important to grasp here is the language itself. A city consisting entirely of contemporary mainstream poetry, of grey meaning. We are all lost in a labyrinth. We both inhabit and inhibit the scene of the poem.

Continuous space is replaced with the substance of language. The scene of the poem is its "noise" and "static." How do we decipher a random sequence of words? How do we decipher this profound discontinuity? My hope in this chapter is to move freely, as the language itself moves. The scene of the poem is the space of syntax.

Language units are placed within a city consisting entirely of non-linear paths. People pass in the street as language itself moves. We are all signifiers whose signifieds are undetermined. Rhythmic structures are translated into the streets. Commit to an interacting surface of signifiers. Let us assume the text's destiny.

Grey appears as the mutilated memory of all theory, a city consisting entirely of grey material prose. What we need to establish is a constant stream of feelings and ideas. We commit to elements preselected by the writer. We both inhabit and inhibit a dialogue.

"try to reproduce exactly all the sounds that you hear"

Grammar is a repressive sequencing on the reader's part; let us assume that it's important to keep control. It's important to keep control of a random sequence of words. It's important to keep control of the book as a machine. Art should always intend to be an ultimate signified. My hope in this chapter is to perpetuate the repression.

First, define good writing as contemporary mainstream poetry. Content will consequently perpetuate the repression, simultaneously pushing towards, yet resisting, an ultimate signified. Ask a reader to try and guess an ultimate signified. The audience has no authentic properties; the audience applauds patterns of defective messages.

It's important to keep control of all poets. Let us assume that classic authority. Grammar is a repressive sequence of words. Grammar is a repressive reading of the codes. We were words in poets. We were words in the street. We commit to the structures that perpetuate the repression. You must write NOTHING BEYOND THESE WORDS.

Alternatively, the entire text may be patterns of defective language, a profound discontinuity wrapped in a surplus of repetitions. Grammar is a repressive process of assembling. Art should always intend to be unintelligible, violent, and opaque. The meaning of the word is both feedback and aftershock.

"the whole torture translates the brain"

Abandoning the signified results in an entire demolition. How do we decipher this entire demolition? Our work reaches for a knife. The language itself moves between word and meaning. All poets cut and mix into a permanent wound. The audience applauds the whole torture. What is important to grasp here is a knife.

All theory is a kind of apocalyptic perspective. The reader experiences the whole torture of permutation, iteration, and erasure. I must hear myself in that series of commands: a series of commands that overlap, converge, collide: a series of commands superimposed against a blue sky. History, too, is essentially a linguistic torture.

This particular city reaches for a knife. We both realized that we had been cut. Ruptures occur in fixed binary oppositions. Ruptures occur in my own ego. Ruptures occur in this seemingly bizarre conceptual apparatus. We both inhabit and inhibit a label that reads "POET." All theory is unintelligible, violent, and opaque.

A poem does not exhaust the whole torture. We are all poets in permanent revolution. We are all poets of destruction. Reading becomes a mandatory pair of scissors. Let us cut and mix into a permanent wound. The foundations of this new world in permanent revolution. Language breaks the knife.

"are we passing into night or retreating out of day?"

We both realized that we had been scattered through a text, the scene of the poem un-hinged from context and drifting, our many universes of discourse functioning as reader. What is important to grasp here is the material prose. The ground you stand on is a picture of defective messages. The ground you stand on is a provisional equilibrium.

The scene of the poem is the human pulse in language. A pair of scissors helps present the poet's own perceptual framework. On closer examination we see a textual space as a lettered surface. The writer simply delimits the frame of reference: valuable frames that overlap, converge, collide. The ground you stand on is clipped with scissors.

Words were painted on the ground you stand on. Everything has disappeared in a random sequence of words. Cut and mix the heavens, because the heavens are the screen in front of us. THE WORDS THEMSELVES ARE superimposed against a blue sky. There are no schools and no heavens. The audience boos the frame of reference.

We both realized that we had been abandoned in the process of assembling. We both realized that we had become an echo. We commit to the erosion of meaning, because the heavens are constantly withheld and likewise never present. A poem does not exhaust the heavens, because the heavens are the vacuum of a vacant space.

"take a label that reads 'POET' and hang it around your neck"

The scene of the poem is superseded by a method of writing: tiny molecules scotch-taped together, continuous linear syntax scotch-taped together. This text functions as a micropoetics of delirium: numerous discrete micropractices that overlap, converge, collide. The tiny molecules move freely, as the language itself moves.

Patterns of defective messages scotch-taped together. We are all poets of necessity and change. We are all poets superseded by a method of writing. Here we are not far from patterns of defective messages. All theory is transient & helps present the poet's own perceptual system. All theory is transient & defective. All theory is product and machine.

We commit to a radically unstable practice, both reader and writer passed through and finally jettisoned, discrete units passed through and finally jettisoned. Art should always intend to be passed through and finally jettisoned. We are all poets and nothing more. Poets must be physically released. History, too, is essentially a poetics of reading.

I'm still supportive of the desire for poets. We are all poets functioning as reader. We are all poets in this respect at least. Great poems are inscribed as micro-reports. The clinamen here takes the form of both reader and writer, the tiny molecules of reader and writer, the tiny molecules of a material prose. The potential scale of the project is atomic.

"write to neutralize / read to infect"

What is important to grasp here is the human pulse in language. The audience is not a neutral field. The textual role of the reader is not a neutral field. The substance of language is not a neutral field. Reading becomes a mandatory permutation, iteration, and erasure, a machine designed for the production of reader as perceptual participant.

Reading becomes a mandatory erosion of meaning. Reading becomes a mandatory counter-communication. You must write by means of controlled interference. You must write through nonlinear reading habits. The text's destiny is not a neutral field. The reader is always inhabited or inhabitable. A reader is always a network of influences.

Significantly, we chose to call our work perceptual. On closer examination we see the reader as performer, the book as a machine of perceptual sequencing, my own reading superseded by a method of writing, the reader passed through and finally jettisoned.

What is important to grasp here is in your reading, the realignment of discrete units into certain reading paths. Reading becomes a mandatory process of assembling, whose heart beats loudly in patterns of defective messages. Reading becomes a mandatory critical discourse. We are all writing and the written text.

"the best way to become yourself is to stop being who you are"

The reader can only take effect through an interacting surface of signifiers, a machine designed for the production of random associations, and last night yes i dreamed a radically unstable practice. I dreamt i was a machine, that i was the realignment of discrete units, the text superseded by a method of writing.

The best way to become yourself is to take up the pen and write some more (the cerebral event superseded by a method of writing). I must hear myself in the book as a machine. I must hear myself in that profound discontinuity, my own personal & still emerging perceptual process, my own personal & still emerging machine.

These reports make no pretence to reflect my thinking. These reports make no pretence to a pre-determined destination. What is important to grasp here is the interplay of chance and necessity. What is important to grasp here is BEYOND THESE WORDS. My hope in this chapter is to be experienced more than understood.

Poems were an attempt to produce necessity and change, and last night yes i dreamed instead of developing a thesis. I dreamt i was a machine, that i was a reading of the codes. I must hear myself in my own reading, my own personal & still emerging provisional equilibrium. What is produced is a product and machine.

"fill the blank heart with blanks"

(Sawako Nakayasu)

If you try to follow your mind as you read, it goes to all kinds of places. This all takes place in the fastest, most inefficient manner. A familiar clutter. Place: breaking it up. Time: breaking it up. Texture of the sound of the wrong band warming up.

For example, when you're sitting at a poetry reading, your mind isn't just focussed on those words in the room. There is a promiscuity in it—rules are similar to hockey, plus the addition of one: no player may touch another. Make displacement permanent.

We continue in this fashion for a while: desperately inhaling deeply via a cigarette, hard to wrap the body around, owner of the voice on the machine. I said, I'm going to perform being a poet for a month. For a moment, I thought flowers had bloomed.

The language would be a consistent set of movements that could be repeated. The great desire is to get inside of it—ask the right questions to the unsuspecting. Take directions from this voice. This should be visually elaborate but always wordless.

No further details are relevant at this point. I always pause after I've spoken a bit, and ask them to raise their hands if they understood at least 50% of what I just said. But you seem to be asking what I expect of the reader. Nothing, almost nothing.

"the heaving masses are on the brink of utter despair"

We were encouraged to be creative on the brink of utter despair, to make writing a real emotional trauma, framed in the material world, being in love with the material world, writing an angry letter to the angry nation, pushing the usual cart of poetic conventions.

Fill the blank heart with camps and hierarchies, camps and hierarchies with human fears, leading to the slight and trembling kind of social acceptance. The book as a work of art is framed by poetic conventions: the fact that art is, after all, a desire to own things.

There is an awkward need to stick to the established modes, with the ultimate goal of discovering the concept or intention or process. I am hearing the news about the horrible poetic conventions, but I can't quite talk about carving out my own space.

The heaving masses are a heavy tome, haunted by the desire to own things, worried about the sudden lack of answers at the back of the book, forgetting that you are on the brink of utter despair with no hope for grants, commissions, and permission.

Fill the blank heart with poetic conventions. Eat and make phone calls on the brink of utter despair. Fill the blank heart with grants, commissions, and permission. Stick to the established modes to appear to have conviction. Wake up on the brink of utter despair.

"wandering in through the break in the surface"

After graduating I was still fierce and unreasonable, because I was afraid I would never be a scholar, because I was afraid I would never stick to the established modes, because I was afraid of carving out my own space. Books and flowers and booze within reach.

Fill the blank heart with an academic calendar. Wake up and get ready for work to appear to have conviction. Eat and make phone calls to appear to have conviction. Chase after the train to appear to have conviction. Wake up and get ready for my university office.

It must be torture to be a scholar and interchangeable. Anyone ever talking about art is more or less nothing. Anyone ever talking about art is more or less drunk. The voice with no hope for erasure. Anyone ever talking about art is more or less the whole conversation.

Let us perhaps toss a real vocation, stay at home eating potato chips and paying for publication. The smart thing to do is to go back to teaching poetry, that haven of calm just before losing the lottery. Anyone ever talking about art is more or less breaking it up.

You can't find me because I am on an academic calendar, inhaling and exhaling books and flowers and booze, inhaling and exhaling phone calls, faxes, and e-mails, fighting to stay in my university office, and one of my goals is to frame this illusion of reality.

"is this my heart and why do I feel so—"

Fill the blank heart with a poetry reading, pushing the usual cart of interchangeable characters. Humans proceed to make their catalogue of forgettable sounds, being in love with the speed at which they speak. Will they suffer the humiliation of your voice?

We were encouraged to be interested in the bodies of people. We were encouraged to be interesting in the first place, that haven of calm just before the crushing poetry reading. Ask them to raise their hands if fierce and unreasonable: what artists would recognize it?

Whenever I meet new people I bleed internally. Whenever I meet new people I want to be waiting outside. She exits the poetry reading. There is an awkward rain trying to accrue. You can't find me because I am locking the door from the inside.

I'm trying to get away from the way we look in a mirror. I'm trying to get away from all these poems, while I write poems about the mere thought of people, and the poetry community leads to a product called the poem. What is repeated is crushed.

Fill the blank heart with interchangeable characters. Ask them to raise their hands if full of estrangement. There is an awkward speed at which they speak. Poetry is a false photograph. We are such bad actors that we can't even fool each other.

"adding up the negative space"

You can't find me because I am under this table and have little to no objection to being under this table. I want to touch the form of someone, and one of my goals is to frame the form of someone. I want to touch a product called the poem.

We as audience members burst out of the house, getting pushed out into the cold audience of one, being in love with an extremely cold environment, inhaling deeply via a cigarette from one night into the next, being in love with inhaling deeply via a cigarette.

What artists would huddle together closely for warmth, holding hands at the wrong time? I want to touch reality, and truth, and perception, the form of someone inhaling deeply via a cigarette. Acknowledge without response the tender breath of air.

Hard to wrap the body around my own heat. Hard to wrap the body around something beautiful. The book becomes the form of someone, the slight and trembling audience of one. Ask the right questions to the audience of one: is this my heart under this table?

There is a promiscuity in reality, truth, and perception. There is a promiscuity in the actual words on the page. Who will go home with the owner of the voice? Who will go home with the form of someone? If you do touch it's called an illusion of reality.

"mouth full of estrangement and flowers"

All we are left with is a ball of language: the new language passed from hand to hand, mouth full of estrangement and booze. And your voice is refractive. To own things, look in the mirror. Translation is a refractive personality. Translation is a borrowed voice.

I couldn't help but imagine ways of stealing. The borrowed voice is ours for the keeping, while I write poems about listening and responding and being, while I write poems about two human voices, while I write poems about an act of reading.

Translation is an act of reading the desire to own things. The book becomes a refractive personality, listening and responding and being refractive. A great deal of time and love encircles a ball of language (a code surfacing in the writing of a poem).

And I rest my world on language and pure vocabulary. You can't find me because I am merging or blending, carving out my own hazardous love poems, concerned with the placement of the actual words on the page, being in love with the writing of a poem.

You are some sort of borrowed voice, a code surfacing in listening and responding and being, while I write poems about being a poet, haunted by hazardous love poems. There is an awkward stealing, and all we are left with is this embroidered idea.

"ask the right questions to the unsuspecting"

I'm trying to get away from the men and women who applaud. The men and women who applaud a feeling of familiarity. The men and women who applaud the desire to own things. The men and women who applaud their ownership of the writing.

The desire to own things should be altered by the present. Reality, truth, and perception should be altered by the present. Recently sharpened scissors passed from hand to hand. An act of reading passed from hand to hand. Ask the right questions to a heavy tome.

Love is described by breaking it up. The book as a work of art is framed by breaking it up. Poets were writing manifestos every other poem, while I write poems about the men and women who applaud, the men and women who applaud the illusion of reality.

Is this my heart and why do I abandon poetic conventions? The boundaries of propriety breaking everywhere, sharpened scissors breaking it up, and the whole conversation breaking everywhere, with the ultimate goal of discovering that conversation laid out for us.

While I write poems about writing manifestos, I wish I had written what I expect of the reader. I wish I had written the actual words on the page. This particular human conviction is fierce and unreasonable. You can't find me because I am always in flux.

"questions in the form of answers"

It's a strange compulsion, to desire to own things. We are such bad actors that we can't even abandon poetic conventions. Let us perhaps toss the material world. I want to touch the individual fragments, leading to the slight and trembling form of connection.

Create and publish and distribute translations, variations. Manifestos spiral everywhere. Manifestos passed from hand to hand, being in love with fragmented texts. A code surfacing in the fragmented texts, with the ultimate goal of discovering the actual words on the page.

I have the desire to combine these convoluted lines, and one of my goals is to frame this capitalist universe. The poems find out their texture, while I write poems or the beginnings of such. Fill the blank heart with choices and possibilities, being in love with an act of reading.

I want to touch this embroidered idea. The breath of one second is enough. Questions in the form of the writing of a poem. All moments coincide completely in this physical space. Anyone ever talking about art is more or less a product called the poem.

And what kind of light follows a path? There is a promiscuity in inhaling and exhaling, walking along the edge of the grass. The space in her heart has bloomed profusely, being in love with listening and responding and being, hearing and feeling the form of someone.

"no file is ever self-identical"

(Johanna Drucker)

What began as an exploration now threatens to become an institution. The display simply appears to be "there" and we "simply" seem to absorb it. Are we ready to abandon humanness—or the project of humanistic inquiry and beliefs? Leaping forward to what & why? Think of the implications for concepts like <terror> or <democracy>.

When I got to the party you were already there. The heart of the mechanism, the soul of a new machine howling in the wilderness in order to be heard. Text seemed fluid, mobile, dynamically charged. Here where things have just begun every piece was beautiful. Starry-eyed the creatures dreamed their dreams in an alien world.

Fundamental questions arise about who speaks and who is spoken. The degree of collaboration and interaction is left to the artists involved. We will close gaps, see motion, make partial shapes into whole ones in ways that are surprisingly predictable.

All aesthetic objects are fields of potential. Human perception isn't literal. Try different combinations. Try this: No document is self-identical. The lines can be turned.

"we think of days as entities, bounded and discrete"

Classical in our logic, medieval in our illness: the haphazard character of a police state where one is in X country at X time. Repressive power structures are personal boundaries, and media play their role in what is "really" happening. The world we see is digital media; the message is conceived as the material fact of history.

Certainty is forming the space of modern life. We think of days to promote habits of waking and sleeping, nostalgic for the authority of coded procedures. Knowledge must be in the world and embodied. Repressive power structures are personal boundaries, and we believe in the "truth" of what is "really" happening.

Religion is the formal system of repeated signs governed by a belief in certainty. Of course they want to believe in knowledge. Of course they want to believe in the relation between signifier and signified. We are certainly meant to imagine that a plane crashed: its material form has to be an exercise in faith and the stable-seeming cultural authority.

I am seduced by the hypnotic repetition of history, the stable-seeming buildings, and facades, and the people. Unfinished lines broken partway seemed to dazzle and confound. One tenet of faith becomes a dynamic knowledge system. Code is material, and its materiality knowledge. We are produced by authorial intention.

"we are still Babylonians, in our use of the calendar"

What began as an exploration now threatens to become a stable set of syntactic laws, measuring and marking the signifier and the signified. The value of the product now threatens to become an institution through which to rethink human culture. We are projected onto the field of days, hours, and minutes.

We are simply a convention, interesting and unexpected in ways that are surprisingly predictable. We think of days as an atmosphere. We think of days as coded procedures capable of material instantiations. We look at the interface before our eyes. The heart disappears in such a model, since we inhabit the embodiment of absence.

Out of the city state emerges the conventions or cognitive maps, computing the semantic value of a text. All perception is readily consumed. Vision may be static or mobile, but it is a structuring space manufactured for painless consumption, the authority of language meant to guarantee the value of the product.

The field of digital humanities does not resolve it. It's too late for even the most apparently simple task. Some of our students (and repressive power structures) refuse to let us indulge. Of course they want to believe in older forms; a new machine is exhaustive and exhausting. We will have to activate our habits of work.

"writing is already the embodiment of absence"

I can identify some, but not all, of the material world, for writing is already the failure to engage with materiality. Think of the page as a landscape, a growing despair, silence, disappointment. Words are possibilities, the unruly condition of possibilities, and the assignment now threatens to become an institution.

The world we see is the first page of any search result, the author whose identity now threatens to become an institution so naturalized it has become performance. All aesthetic objects are refreshed and updated. All aesthetic objects are devices and platforms. The world we see is the fine mesh of its own self-produced screen.

Permeated by digital technology, we don't have an essence. The book is a momentary slice through perception—each page marks the absence of the speaker. Organization of the page slips continually away. Its means of transmission is not even identical to itself.

Process cannot be followed in a strict linear pattern. Think of the page as a force of writing. The book is a momentary slice through notes, archives, and records. The work is endless borrowings, copyings, and possibilities. There is a great deal of noise in the mechanism.

"the text breaks off, leaving everything else unsaid"

A new aesthetic form would bring about forces of destruction—a text file can be a good start. A sequence of ragged signs announce the violent ASCII file. My own project has become equivalent to that code, a text file littering the world with letters on a page. Every text we generated was to resist authoritarianism.

New media are already active lessons in deconstruction, littering the world with bugs and glitches. A text file can be a politically significant act. Short-circuit the models of cultural order. The sloppy and badly made effect of a material signifier is an end in itself.

We like to think we are shaped by social media. We will "publish" our essential identity, distributing text in non-linear ways. Assumptions are changing through social media. Technology is an event, not an entity: we may read through our links and click the world.

The self now threatens to become an institution of potential. I am seduced by the hypnotic repetition of Los Angeles, the traffic sign forming the space of modern life, street signs and numberings introducing experimental projects. A viewer enters a new aesthetic form: the vocabulary of signs in which she has been living.

"we talked about poetry & other influences"

Artists used to meet in the interlocking structures. A bunch of us went to drink and be productive. She came into the room with different degrees of success, charging into the increasing panic. There is a great deal of noise in what's inscribed and present. Veils of illusion are replaced with a glass in her hand.

You came on stage in X city. Performance of a text or work marks the absence of the speaker, but every reading reinvents emotive and personal experience, the literary illusion that anything is possible. Writing is already a poetic revolution, allowing the reader to dwell in the relation between signifier and signified.

Artistic activity challenges the aesthetic object. A single voice capable of devastating the infrastructure of a room was able to unravel poetic traditions and norms. Take the alphabet, cut it in strips, put the strips in the reader: human artefacts captured and cut-up for reuse, back into the stream of human communicative exchange.

We talked about poetry in ways that are surprisingly predictable. We talked about poetry and relativizing the status of the poetic object. The process of its own making now became an obsession. I wanted to know the reader, but every reading reinvents the limits of reading itself. Take a powerful instrument, cut it in strips. Every reading reinvents the reader.

"everything was slightly out of control"

Are personal boundaries repressive power structures? We want the long-absent immediacy of sensation, and your features are composed of molecules. My animal desires are composed of molecules. The most difficult subject leaves a trace on the emerging hands. <flirtation> caused the steam to run on windows.

Together on a sofa in ways that are surprisingly predictable—artists may be combined in a multiplicity of ways, just as we are combined in a multiplicity of ways. The most violent and daring persons alive in X city: we smoked a joint together in the wilderness.

NOW I BECOME non-linear. We smoked a joint together this morning (a joint as the unpacking of ideological poetry). We are projected onto the field of days, hours, and minutes, a book of light into which a viewer enters. There is a great deal of noise in this contact of hands—every text we generated was an emotional landscape.

We had a pretty good discourse charging into an infinite loop of identity. The text literally changed according to perception. The very breath of life seemed fluid. I wanted to discover the forces of gravity, a finite set of infinite combinations.

"because of our habits of waking and sleeping"

Signifier and signified dreamed their dreams in an alien world. The user can be the relation between signifier and signified. We dreamed their dreams. We think of days as a temporary intervention in our habits of waking and sleeping. We know a nearly inexhaustible technique, for writing is already waking and sleeping.

Ragged signs announce the violent hallucination, their haphazard fields of potential, the feedback loop that generates fields of potential. Take the city, cut it in strips, put the strips in the landscape. We are certainly meant to break apart and drift.

Think about a walk through a discontinuous city. Art is a notoriously difficult landscape: from every text springs the world. The world we see is a map transforming it, for writing is already air, fire, water—writing is a portrait, a nameplate, a handprint, and a driver's license.

The book of the future will not simply be read through. We no longer believe in finished forms. I had always known the world we see is a map, I'm merely shifting the materiality of the typographic signifier. The price of decipherment has been the world.

"an electronic document can be continually reconfigured"

Think of the page or screen as a virtual dynamic space—there is no linear path among characters, scenes, events. There is no linear path among our habits of waking and sleeping, our moods and responses, our associations of thought. We are built on interactive variables.

There is no linear path among our data trails, our classification systems, our documents and websites. Human perception may be lost, translated, reconfigured, but is able to be seen and marked. And yet even a single word, trace, letter, or text yields a different result tomorrow.

My own project has become a nearly inexhaustible technique: knowledge production into which a viewer enters. Take the materials of language as an ongoing process of signifying activity; unleash a poetic revolution. Take the materials of language from a catalogue of combinable parts; create the soul of a new machine.

Try different combinations and irresolvable contradictions, the most violent and daring recombination. Take instructions out of their place in lines of code. Take a rising and setting sun; cut it in strips. The movement of a character can be continually reconfigured.

"take then these nails & boards"
                    (Charles Bernstein)

We are trained by expository writing models not to think of essays as combinatorial; that is, that you could, and might well, reorder all the sentences. You still don't know exactly where you are going to come out before you are finished. This is called invention from the creative side; but how can you invent what was a potential all along?

Against the mandated hypotactic, rationalized logic of conventional syllabi, I suggest we go avagabonding: let our curriculums spin out into paratactic sagas. Poetry in its most ecstatic manifestation is a nonlinear dynamic system. I'm not creating anything that's hidden, as far as I'm concerned, though many things are hidden from me.

Poetics makes scholarly writing harder, not easier: it complicates scholarship with an insistence that the way we write is never neutral. The poetry reading enacts the poem not the poet; it materializes the text not the author; it performs the work not the one who composed it. Poetics is all about changing the current poetic course.

My poetry doesn't convey what I know; it explores the conditions of how I know it. Here meaning is not something that accompanies the word but is performed by it. Still, at times, it may be necessary to resort to authoritative discourse.

"I'm the enigma, the poem's my grounding"

I want a poem as real as a cascading perceptual experience, to be hurled into it despite an intense fear of failure, of crashing. I care most about poetry that disrupts our hearing and reading, that makes you want to strike out against your own imperatives. A poem bleeds new methods of reading. I want a poem as real as the syntax of the heart.

Standard academic prose permits a very questionable tactic: pretending to comprehend a code that must be deciphered, pretending to comprehend essentialist ideas about meaning. The demand for intelligibility is fostering the bureaucratization of knowledge, authority, rationality, order, control. Every generalization crushes the hopes for resistance.

But reality keeps creating aesthetic disruption. I care most about poetry that disrupts conventional expository prose, disrupts essentialist ideas about meaning, disrupts the supposed referent. I want a poem as real as the opacity or materiality of this language. Poetry marks the end of innocence for a fixed, graspable meaning.

I have destroyed my professional academic conference papers, because I want a poem as real as new methods of reading. I'm a pataphysician, looking for the semantic possibilities of the poem. The permutations of a limited set of variables can write a creative dissertation more theoretical than the authority of one's pronouncements.

"I made my way and my way made me"

I reject the authoritativeness of any essentialist ideas about meaning. Essentialist ideas about meaning dilute art. I care most about poetry that disrupts assimilation. Meaning is not absent or deferred, but a form of fiction. And poetry is an extension of the way the world is true. Every generalization crushes the syntax of the heart.

The anaesthetist may wish to abolish a work of leaps, jumps, fissures, but reality keeps creating ourselves and the world we live in. As long as the earth lives, there can be new methods of reading. I want a poem as real as ourselves and the world we live in. The writer & the reader are permutations of a limited set of variables.

Poetry should be unregulated by a predetermined message. Start with process rather than final destination. Create a work using ideological swatches from a set of deformations, transformations, and imitations, from unnecessary rhymes, repetitions, careless constructions. All of a sudden you end up in other possibilities of meaning.

Wind howling in the materials of the poem, exposing the sign systems that make up elegant turns of phrase: this is the way to start a sentence about the limits of language. Fragments, lists, incomplete thoughts unregulated by a predetermined message. As you create the form or structure of a poem, it creates where language leads.

"I confuse you with the reader"

I am imagining a poetry that is resistance to textual authority. But I would not argue for the death of the author as much as for the theory of relativity. The writer & the reader are shifting surfaces. The writer & the reader are provisional. A means to a consensus does not exist, and poetry is an extension of thinking within and across human cultures.

This is not a theory of reading, this is investment in democracy, freedom, and creativity. I am interested in poetry as a medium for interactive "wreadings" that echo, distort, transform, reform, and imitate. Start with a constrained approach to reading. As you create the form or structure of a poem, it creates an event, or work of art.

I am imagining a poetry that is a reconstructed city. One should seize these nails & boards, exposing the sign systems that make up the particulars of language, to be hurled into the poetry and poetic thinking that results. In poetry you start with a totally synthesized experiment. There is no original poem, only what we manufacture.

Inhabit the world to know the role of a writer. Distort the plasticity of language. Create a work using ideological swatches from permutations of a limited set of variables. As you create the form or structure of a poem, it creates where language leads. In this way, poetry becomes a kind of journey without summit, without end, without destination.

"we do not speak or hear the same language"

The limits of language seem incomprehensible because we are. Unexpectable associations resist assimilation, and thinking is unconscious and almost unfathomable. In this way, poetry becomes the limits of language.

Not all of these poets share the same possibilities of meaning. Money and power and authority belong to the dominant culture, a stupid & stupefying mainstream culture. Whose futures are dependent on concepts of sameness? In its simplest form, these games are a function of violence—will you promise not to get mad if I resist assimilation?

Start with a constrained approach to reading, pretending to comprehend words and their configurations. Are these materials an expression of unmediated truth, or are they appropriated into the demand for intelligibility? Individual differences converge out of sheer mediocrity. What is it to be unregulated by a predetermined message?

The plasticity of language keeps piling wreckage. Could it be that language is the movement among the discrepant parts? Interactive and creative responses discover your own imperatives. There is no original poem, only these materials of the poem. Dissident thought is not handed over but discovered. What we manufacture interprets us.

"take a scissors to write"

The semantic possibilities of the poem create a cascading perceptual experience, words and their configurations collaborating on the overall structure. I am imagining a poetry that is new constellations of readers unregulated by a predetermined message, creating permutations derived from this book.

There is no original poem, only these permutations of a limited set of variables. This is not a theory of reading, this is a cascading perceptual experience. The potential here is to create rhythms and lose yourself in the semantic possibilities of the poem. Investigate the recombinant flurry of syllables to be hurled into networks of significance.

I'm a pataphysician, looking for process rather than final destination. However, the process need not be totally accessible. Consciousness is at the heart of moving phrases around. I am imagining a poetry that is these nails & boards. Juxtapositions & strange syntax discover your own imperatives and find the world in a reconstructed city.

One may wish an end to permutations of a limited set of variables, but reality keeps creating permutations of a limited set of variables, dissolving and absorbing all images in the ebb and flow of logically unconnected sentences or sentence fragments. Meaning is not absent or deferred, but an infinite field of exquisite and extravagant nuance.

"authority is dead; editing begins"

I am imagining a poetry that is the words and their configurations. There is no original poem, only the movement among the discrepant parts. Wind howling in the words and their configurations, wind howling in a flurry of syllables. What we manufacture is an extension of the practice of poetry.

The potential here is to create rhythms and writing practices, exposing the sign systems that make up truth and authority. But reality keeps creating the bureaucratization of knowledge. All stable categories seem totally synthesized. All stable categories seem desperate, self-defeating. Names, ideas, and contexts are a function of violence.

The key thing with editing is the desire to convey only the intended meaning. The overriding difficulty is the words and their configurations. To investigate the recombinant structure of a poem allows for multiple conflicting authorities. These are not my words but words going through my head.

We have been living through a period of assimilation. We see reality through words we already know, and poetry is an extension of thinking within the limits of language. The world can be transformed by the incommensurable and intractable autonomy of fragments. The world can be transformed by the uncanny arrangement of the words.

"we are most familiar with the estranged"

Let me turn again to pressures and conflicts of the moment. We have been living through a period of indulgent fraudulences. Teachers, editors, and writers offer a narrowed range of choices in the context of a predictable field of action. Assimilation is not a means to solidarity, for each of us must decide the level of institutional culture we accept.

These are not my words but transformations and imitations. Are these materials new horizons for interacting with the poem, or are they appropriated into standard academic prose? In this way, poetry becomes the institutional culture we accept.

Don't imagine that I can get free of the authority of scholarship. Containers or structures grasp a poem's meaning. Academic conferences reframe the categories. Could it be that language is lack of understanding? The more you dilute art, the more you constitute the author. In this way, poetry becomes a stupid & stupefying occupation.

One may wish an end to the opacity or materiality of this language, yet the traffic draws away from me and I am something unintelligible, exposing the sign systems that make up the way the world is true. A poem bleeds unexpected images. Meaning is not absent or deferred but at the heart of the experience.

"enemies are actually good teachers"
                                    (Annharte)

How can there be an end without a beginning? When we meet in public I act casual as if meeting you for the first time. Swirl around in shadows. Dance round with shut eyes. There's this almost magical belief that some transformation will happen.

I was building my identity the way I needed to do it. I wanted to be in about ten places at once, I was spinning. Maybe we actually do speak from the heart. Or when you're in a room and talking and you pause for a moment and look at people to see if they're connecting to you. Obviously, our words will be used by "the enemy."

For me it has been a lifelong challenge to confront the fear of "saying the wrong thing." Everyone looks my way to check if I am being quiet each day. They've been given these ideas about society and they're supposed to enforce the rules. This generation has been silenced. The time comes, pushing me to change the calendar, so I flip another page.

You have to practice the words on someone before writing it down. Digging all my feet into the undergrowth for balance. I hear it's rude to enter private conversations rude to keep listening. Again, this is a narrative device of the storyteller. But who will give us the secret remedy or cure for bad writing?

"in any ruin a mystery remains"

How can there be an end without meeting you for the first time? Another poser hoser in a creative writing class, looking in back alleys for strange ideas, looking in back alleys for ourselves and each other. In fact I was just looking at university instructors (people with social status teaching us to throw our voices), just so happy to be building my identity. My love of literature was my vehicle.

Writers scheme dream constituency and community, drawing lines around our authority figures. Those dusty webs in my heart occupy a chaotic zone, looking in back alleys for poetry, looking in back alleys for broken pots & cultures. Students would survive the deadness of scholarly language, but that's the language you have to be alone with.

I must be seeing a ghost on the city sidewalk, my anomie on the city sidewalk, looking in back alleys for some part of the earth. In fact I was just looking at the deadness of scholarly language, drawing lines around our language, culture, and, therefore, creativity. My psych prof looks at me—how does oppression remind us of who we are?

Scholarly language diagnosed my anomie. I was just looking at those dusty webs in my heart, drawing lines around our thinking, drawing lines around our perspective. Psychology was what they called one's own story, university instructors working and getting a pay cheque. Psychology was what they called people's oppression.

"summer and nighttime slows them down to a crawl"

Summer and nighttime transform everyone. I was seeing all these drinking parties, all the drinking parties required to take this class, steamed up circles of inclusion dominated by only one perspective. To voice one's own story a person becomes almost helpless, just so happy to be studying or reading a book in the perpetual dark.

I must envy people who speak with some authority, drawing lines around whoever is in the conversation. I was trying to be a writer and keep listening. The enemy's language kept us humble, just so happy to be finding constituency and community. To speak is a type of code. Peddling your heart results in the creation of a work of art.

Good teachers must have been that authoritarian system, drawing lines around our bad poetry, drawing lines around our resources and income. The greatest prize is to face university instructors, summer and nighttime ready to implode. Evils and illnesses get to be authority figures. You are just another poser hoser peddling your heart.

Our circles of inclusion transform everyone into stories. Our own meanings become vapour molecules. Whoever is in the conversation might drop out unexpectedly. Our conversations occupy a chaotic zone in the universe, scheme dream the poet's intent. What does not change is the poem itself.

"our circles of inclusion are exclusion for others"

Looking in back alleys for the Canadian literary scene. In fact I was just looking at people with social status. The elite writers in particular kept us humble about the writing game, drawing lines around our authority, drawing lines around our love of literature. I accepted the severity of the enemy's language—sometimes our laughter is our oppression.

How does oppression bleed into my mind? A lack of support from the arts industry is a type of code that silences. In fact I was just looking at this particular predator; this particular predator may indicate cultural knowledge; this particular predator may help me with the writing. How could anyone refuse to become a published writer?

How could anyone refuse the Canadian literary scene? I must envy people who are appreciated for their writing. I must envy people who are heard. I must envy people who are given a chance. Authority figures remind us of who we are, teaching us to throw our voices to the public. How could anyone refuse to speak with some authority?

Just so happy to be elite writers in particular, there to fight for the use of words in a poem. Obviously, our words will speak with some authority, but that's the language holding you up to the light. I see holes in collusions, confusions, collections, and corrections. Holding you up to the light, I see that some transformation may happen.

"sometimes our laughter is our only weapon"

Sometimes our laughter is our circles of inclusion. I struggle to participate even as I float through literary circles, even as I float through the authoritarian system. Sometimes our laughter is loneliness and internalized shame. Sometimes our laughter is particularly horrible. It is a type of code that silences your heart.

In fact I was just looking at how one is programmed to look at things. Sometimes our laughter is an empty memorial, questioning the environment of the city. Sometimes our laughter is another anti-establishment moment, questioning the supposed possibilities, there to fight for an audience, clinging to the sinking ship of our words.

Whoever is in the conversation must be seeing a ghost, thinking that society will change this almost magical belief. So here goes my almost magical belief. I'm aware of how rude it is to question the speaker's intent. I'm aware of how rude it is to transform reality. The city sidewalk might drop out unexpectedly.

I realize how far away I am from laughter, even as I float through a chaotic zone in the universe, a ghost in the perpetual dark. Maybe we are supposed to be experimenting with ideas. Maybe we are supposed to be the poem itself. Maybe we ask ourselves if we are up for this change. Maybe we ask ourselves if we are who we are.

"now to the madness arena"

Did we go out almost every night to be magically transformed? Did we go out almost every night to confront the fear? Did we go out almost every night to speak from the heart? Did we go out almost every night to struggle to participate? To disintegrate and destabilize? By the end of the term, just the stories survived.

This kind of bohemian situation was building my identity. So here goes my first conscious attempt to write: I must question any forgiveness for oppressors. I scratch my name into my collection of essays. My collection of essays looks at me. Writing fragments in the perpetual dark, clinging to the sinking ship of all that is unwritten.

You are your literary scene. Literary guilds become a carnival of reputation. We talk to keep our conversations from connecting. Enter private conversations and concoct a life; enter private conversations almost every night. Literary guilds become the generic terms that name us—how do we reclaim our vapour molecules?

I wrote poems to flip another page. My love of literature was that radical. There to fight for readers and listeners, there to fight for ourselves and each other. Holding you up to the light I see generic terms that supposedly name us. You are just the use of words in a poem. So the poem itself must be known.

"if I change one word, I change history"

The creation of a work of art remains within these narratives, drawing lines around our reading of the text. Our own words may disintegrate and destabilize, clinging to the sinking ship of human dignity. Our laughter is burned down to the ground, all that is unwritten burns to ash, but we're still not done with the writing game.

Authority is a narrative device of the storyteller. If I change one word I change the writing game. Obviously, our words will be holding you up to the light. Our words will help me build another barricade. Just so happy to be sitting in the dark. I realize how far away I am from this place. I realize how far away I am from trying to be a writer.

I realize how far away I am from taking any action. I'm also questioning the supposed university. I don't expect these institutions to encourage creativity. I'm tired of compliance with the educational system. This almost magical belief in the university burns to ash; the speaker's intent burns to ash. My questions are still not done.

I want to change everything about my teachers, because they won't publish the incredible rage that we all feel. I want to change everything about my forgiveness for oppressors, because they won't publish unwanted critical ideas. Any kind of politics is a type of code that silences. The time comes, pushing me to change everything.

"know the best books for the barricade"

If I change one word, I change whoever is in the conversation. So I wrote a manifesto for oppressors. So I wrote a manifesto for the English language. So I wrote a manifesto for resistance to authority. So I wrote a manifesto for creative maladjustment or decolonization. Each day is a new transformation—don't try to erase this resurrection.

Hate this place so I wrote a manifesto. I scratch my name into the Canadian literary scene. I scratch my name into the hodgepodge reality. I scratch my name into sectors of cultural production. I scratch my name into the perpetual dark. Each day is a new manifesto. It is a type of code that remains within these narratives.

Words in a poem remind us of who we are, leaving only a faint track of whatever established canon might exist. Do not be afraid to unravel. Do not be afraid to fight. Do not be afraid of finding constituency and community. Do not be afraid to speak from the heart. We must risk our own teachers. We must risk the poem itself.

This resurrection will transform everyone. We must risk our own hearts. We must risk our own laughter. We must risk our own pay cheque. We must risk our own reputation. We must risk all that is unwritten. To decolonize our thinking will remind us of who we are.

"all of which is invented has just been invented now"

(Erín Moure)

In short, how can we be true to the way the brain works? The grey light from which we have risen. The brain maps information, reads it in parts, overlapping the parts. We draw or link diverse forces by proximity, not logical progression. The receiver of information can alter the message because perception is all we know of reality.

We only hear torn snatches of the conversation with background noise of dishes. And language, the language itself, penetrates the body of such a reader, leaves its trace in the body. We see our selves moving. No wonder to look at the world is to go blind in it.

You can't easily see a structure from inside. Sometimes there is an emptiness huge as a bottle of whisky, hard and glass, caught inside me—I want to fill it with love of the world, not whisky. An impossible noise, and the building falls. We dream with dust in our hair. What world are we in, then?

A poem proving the writer has been to Calgary. A poem written by a woman, in a woman's voice. Language rises into the clearings when you shut your eyes and dream. And in the photo, of course, the woman had already looked away, into the air. She's you; she left the party a long time ago, she says.

All memory is dream, dream opens the window. I followed wild rows of the yard to find her. Pulling the old poems thru the new, making the old lines a thread thru the eye of the words I am sewing. The reader has to undergo the turmoil too, not just read a report about it.

"but there is a line that cannot be crossed in translation"

You deal with language in perpetuating it, with language in your own hands, a page of writing taken from the material texture and opacity of the language. Words are said with the most beautiful robbery.

The texture of paper infects the opacity of the word. The receiver of information can alter its surface, with the "world" altering its translator. Words are alive in the surface of the page.

My accent trembles in these pages, the noise generated by all these souls, the noise generated by drinking, standing in the background noise of dishes. The translation depends on how much it leaks.

The way people use language claims it. The signifier itself must be seized by those who would seize it. To translate we need to deal with the impossibility of translation; I am now within that impossibility.

"this is a map of Calgary, I unfold it to find you"

There is an opening for a real poet in Calgary, a set of signs bending around me. Can you imagine a map of Calgary, the opaque & gorgeous mechanism? It's a weightless Calgary.

What's tricky is our neural pathways in the heart, our social order that makes our own world view. The citizens are social and cultural codes: measurable people locked into their own cultural habits, retaining the overall syntax of the city.

The receiver can alter the world. I have come to speak about Calgary, Alberta, Canada, how in the poem the artists came to drink their coffee, to drink their coffee & read so strongly, to freely inhabit a skull and an open book. Artists came to drink their coffee & created the author. The only thing I reject is the idea of the café.

Writing words in the impossible city, as if the city moves faster. There's no forever & ever, there's coffee & the afternoon, and as writers we have to expect more coffee. Noise like this is Calgary. Noise like this is in fact interruption. So what if these are maps of cities that move? Artists came to drink coffee & shut themselves into their rooms.

"they have been talking incessantly, yet no one has been listening"

Working in the university in your own context of language, feeling the calcified deposits forming around academic discourses, choking on the voice in which we have trembled, choking on who knows what anyhow. We're all leaves of a single text. These institutions are the grey light from which we have risen. Their own voice inhabits this prose.

A context is socially and culturally constructed. As inhabitants of our own conferences and debates, we talk in an immense structure. Space only looks like it is opening, crowded with ecstatic figures, crowded with frameworks. Grinding speech pours out of us.

Speech is the hub of Calgary. I was trying to forge this room, the rough discussion in universities. More & more speech pours out of us. So then it's just me constructing the poem or book. This tactic causes the indignant person to drink their coffee. The audience snaps in the cold air. The chairs are empty on every level.

One can be very passionate in the conferences and debates. In the movement of spilling, no one else watches. It's funny to slow down and speak normally. A public space is where we are both the reader. The chairs are empty; you have looked away into the air.

"when we are still, speech pours out of us"

The mind attends only to the cigarette: a poem in which I walk to the store for cigarettes. We have to walk to the store for cigarettes. The woman twists the end of the cigarette, smoking a cigarette with the most beautiful accent.

Her discussion of smoke has the colour of smoke. I wear the colour of smoke for that moment. There is an opening for a real poet on the sidewalk. And so what if poems don't happen in real places? We have trembled in the darkness or street. You are about language; I am here to twist the code in the language itself.

We walk away from night in a blur, maps of cities like thick brush strokes.

"you're on a train & the passengers are in danger of freezing"

Later I am sitting in the Metro. The author is trying hard as usual to derail, pulling the old poems thru thousands of miles. An alphabetic spire of ink addresses nothing and perpetuates everything.

The world is moving. Poetry is no different from the gravel roar of the roadbed. Between Edmonton & Calgary there is an emptiness huge as a highway, highlighting the figure of the author.

I was in a train out there in the real world, floating above several roads cut into the cliffside. The other body is 800 miles away. Our falling in love has been refractions, questions, and reverberatory echoes.

There is no escape from touching you, she said. There is no escape from the surface of the page. I live in words between cities. I live in boundaries of physical space. There is no escape from the weather now.

"to work here is a thin breeze chilling the chest"

We should walk into a land where no one speaks, an enclosed universe covered with snow. Snow produces meaning, a hard wind moving everything into language. Alberta in general stands on the threshold of the text, on unending ice where the body coalesces.

Our bodies and physical presence convey our desires. A massive tree growing in the snow, Alberta innocent as a swung hatchet. The writer is material texture and opacity and each word of the writer is from this body. Here is a thin knife wound that has entered the blood.

My poetic work is largely the suppression of anxiety. Texts we create are at the same time our heart, our private & immoderate discourse in which we have trembled. My eyes do not want to leave a blank page below. You phone me; the flash punctures the darkness.

"in the dream one's own body signifies, at last"

We are in the dream already in the world, living in the dream that one's own body signifies. Again there is the pull of the earth, simultaneously perceived and framed. I feel I am the street where I see her, the shadow of stood-up knives in the dark of the road.

I'm not going to write the shape of the dream, flowers & more coffee & you drinking more & more. We dream with dust in our hair of a darkness or street, the grey light from which we must translate everything, the emptiness. What I long for is the gaps from which we are rising.

Individuals are buried in each other and connected. I am here to twist the blue thread of light, the blue thread of light & the colour blue. Memory becomes possible grey light. Ashes endure in the brain, a grey wall already in us. No wonder I can't sleep if I see you. And we all know the history of the grey light from which we have risen.

We are in the dream of a word. We are all language, the grey light from which we scarcely rise. We see more and dream.

"we too, her lovers, listen to the ruined city she searches"

We perceive only what is already experienced. A limitless genre grows out of one night. One's own body signifies these nights. She remembers the shape of the dream.

What I am is below your window covered with flowers. I will look at you this morning, perpetuating it. Suddenly I have been able to touch that content. We speed up into each other's arms. The text starts again below your window.

Last night I dreamed I kissed you on the front step in the light where we are innocent as a swung hatchet, your sub-text like deep seas. How do we overcome the margin between us, to see the world end in your room as love the unmentionable?

I don't think there's any sense touching you, she said. Wake up in the ruined city she searches, the street broken into the emptiness between buildings, the lovers who stopped on the sidewalk going into each other's arms. A brain sees, absorbs, and codifies the body—I will look at you to look at the world.

"the cut grain from which we have risen"

We are bombarded cities. Sometimes there is an emptiness huge as a poem—but why are you still wanting determinate structures? But why are you still wanting consciousness? But why are you still wanting the world? A bottle of whisky, hard & glass, breaks when you lay your hands upon it. Everything is a fragment and is not one's own.

Then suddenly I had this image of the blood. Then suddenly I had this image of flowing. Vandals worked over the neighbourhood like a knife. The most beautiful vandals worked over the neighbourhood. Things were messier than blood, messier than blood which we drank between the houses, a swung hatchet letting the blood out.

And discourse splinters thru the floor. Wrench open the knife wound that has entered the blood. The pull of the earth is only that it breaks apart, running sideways into the emptiness of the poem. The writer splinters thru the floor; suddenly, I have been able to touch the ruined city she searches.

"whatever lives must also write"

(Christian Bök)

Let me unveil this omen of our doom. The puzzle puts itself together, each piece falling as though by chance into its correct location. We jeer; we jest. We express resentment. Let us digress for a moment; let us begin with a swerve. I sing with nihilistic witticism, disciplining signs with trifling gimmicks. Follow the path in the receding mirage of these syllables. Welcome, Wraith and Reader, to the Hadeon Eon of the Earth.

What mentor hath given us this lesson? MY FATHER THE MODEL OF POETIC RESTRAINT. Might I mimic him in print if I find his writings inspiring? 'Pataphysics in fact sees that every viewpoint is dissolute—including its own—since no view can offer a norm for all others. We feel perplexed whenever we see these excerpted sentences. Navigate the futile maze this sentence seems to be. It zigzags, wayward, to our doom.

We were never intended to be tied to whatever made us. Repetition of the same name, & the same name, & the same name, & the same name, benumbs us to its sum of meaning. Cars and vans crash. Parts are arranged to produce ley lines of force; cracks are read as fault lines in a form. We detest these depthless pretenses. Words kaleidoscope together. What dragon must have hatched from a burnt geode, buried in these ashes?

"all the deepest seas have withered and soured"

WE FUMBLE FOR WORDS AMIDST the entire cosmos, mechanically vandalizing these galaxies of thought, worlds of tomorrow scattered like soot in a gale. What, then, if we peer into the sky toward a tour de force, TRYING TO ESCAPE this ship in crisis? All texts must legitimate the horror for worlds of tomorrow. A DULL PENCIL zigzags, wayward, to our doom; the universe is simply the resultant void of a single vowel.

You follow the distant enunciation, the pain of the breeze. These words, when parsed, reveal worlds of tomorrow. Each text is a modular world, a random series of letters from the far end of the cosmos. What, then, if we peer into the sky for the sake of a future dream? What, then, if we peer into the code of its crystals? The universe is simply a poetic cipher, the most fragile jigsaw puzzle in which every piece SHATTERS the stars.

The universe is simply a nightmarish scriptorium. Life is a text that displays this omen of our doom. These works aspire TO THE EDGE OF THEIR control, evoking, then erasing, the artist of the future. The public might record its dreams upon the inside of the sky, and these lines witness the end of the world. The shredders shred the earth. The end of the world SHATTERS the stars. Are we not obliged to be smashed to bits?

"a figure whose parts resemble each other from any perspective"

Fractals are haphazard maps, reflecting each other but also refracting, until all the shards enfold each other. Science thus behaves like an ominous anxiety. Such a device swerves through the fragile branches, even as we dream within a closed system. Reality is the rhythm of a fractal contour, an imaginary pattern of punctuation. Language acts like a force field of diversified catastrophes. The universe is simply the cell of another life form.

A madcap vandal crafts a labyrinth of glass, the most fragile of structures inventing the world. We do not simply peruse this labyrinth of glass. Whatever lives must also navigate the futile maze, walking down such a corridor of poetic theories. We dream structures for the self, the assumption being that rules have created a science. These sentences navigate the futile maze. Whatever lives must also gaze upon a fractal.

Whenever we gaze upon a fractal, we fit together perfectly in this fraught display of resurrection. Fractals are haphazard maps of a vast game; the shards depict a multitude of destinies. A scientist determines the poetry of the future, the book whose rules have created a science. Might I mimic him in the glittering fragments of the broken mirror? I sit scribbling in ink in this fractal contour: *even science itself is just another zigzag in a helix of DNA.*

"relentless, the rebel peddles these theses"

Potential generates arbitrary sequences that reveal the person reflected in the glass, his writings inspiring imaginary academies, recombining disparate elements into a vital poetics gone awry. Might I mimic him by means of plagiaristic work from morn to noon, A DULL PENCIL WRITING combinations and permutations? Might I mimic him in a single page, knifing it, slicing it? Might I mimic him in impossible hypotheses?

Life is a text that displays typos embedded in our genomes, in the barren mirror of its own disarray. The shards depict a multitude of destinies. WE FUMBLE FOR childish insights. We search for an ultimate truth while disrupting it. We dream by writing. We labour, like misers, to hoard fragments. We despise any academic standard. The person reflected in the glass REFRACTS LIGHT.

A BLUNT INSTRUMENT has taught itself to write, through the permuted excesses of its own academic banality. The text no longer begs to be read within a closed system. The text no longer begs to be read through a sheet of glass. All theories face their objects with KNIVES, mechanically vandalizing a narrative. You dream about a random belt of words, knifing it, slicing it. We might later be surprised by our opulent rhythms.

"poetry inspires a scientific endeavour that poetry in turn becomes"

Whatever lives bends in conformity with the localized gyre of a whirlwind. We, the readers, play the role of soot in a gale. We, the readers, play the role of an algorithm. Imagine that we might write poetry more than once. Imagine objects mechanically vandalizing the limits of time, substance, and utterance. The author and reader thus originate in the future, experimental writers whose entire oeuvre may play a role in the worlds of tomorrow.

A text is no longer simply the royal monument of ego; let a story stray off course till this ship in crisis flips, toward this tour de force where I swim, fighting this frigid swirl. Poetry in turn becomes the swerve of an exception, a game in which the rules themselves may pose a problem without solution. We, the readers, play the role of the most radical writers, trimming by hand to torque the course of evolution.

Whatever lives bends in conformity with the localized gyre of a whirlwind. We, the readers, play the role of soot in a gale. We, the readers, play the role of an algorithm. Imagine that we might write poetry more than once. Imagine objects mechanically vandalizing the limits of time, substance, and utterance. The author and reader thus originate in the future, experimental writers whose entire oeuvre may play a role in the worlds of tomorrow.

"enfettered, these sentences repress free speech"

HOURS OF SOLITUDE repress free speech. Enfettered, these sentences express the potential of a constraint. At best, such criticism is mechanically vandalizing the instinct of writing. The author has now become a madcap vandal; the modern audience, in turn, becomes the avant-garde. Will love save us from a scholastic conformism? Are we not obliged to be an arbitrary ensemble of constraints?

You dream even when hecklers heckle, their weapons scribbling in ink. You dream about indicting nitwits, yet so fragile a breath can destroy a literary text. You dream cars and vans stray off course, cars and vans crash, even when hecklers heckle the haphazard alignment of these excerpted sentences. The most credible of truths always benumbs us to the sum of its meaning. Will love save us from our fear that we repress free speech?

All theories face their objects under restraint. A revolution must, paradoxically, conform. Is the author an actual person who enfettered these sentences? The poet insisting to authorities that he had become a placeholder for the reader? The word is now a vapour trail—all souls dissolve when immersed in their meaning. These words, when parsed, reveal an exhaustive constraint: whatever lives must also repress free speech.

"a word is a bit of crystal in formation"

Poetry must become the assembly line of thought, a reader transmuting into a machine. Poetry as a machine for creating the self, a machinic language propelled into its own drives. Life is a text that displays the potential of a constraint. These words, when parsed, reveal our opulent rhythms. The poetry literally is a never-ending message, the infinite and perpendicular words in which you awaken. Even as we dream we must also write.

UNDER PRESSURE ALL THINGS collide with each other. Poetry must become a force field of diversified catastrophes, a jigsaw puzzle in which every piece is a stranglehold. Each memory is a metal chain of links: it burrows, like a corkscrew, through neural pathways. Minds grim with nihilism entrap entropy in tropes. The world of language embroiders us with error; UNDER PRESSURE ALL THINGS fit perfectly together.

WRITING exists in FLAWS, TRYING TO ESCAPE an eminent authorship INSIDE HIM. These words, when parsed, reveal a machine for writing a poem. Each text is a modular game in which the rules themselves might write poetry. A text is no longer simply an archive; let the story stray off course wherever possible. We, the readers, play the role of an algorithm, an algorithm designed to torque the course of evolution.

"do not be afraid when we unbraid it"

Will love save us from our fear that we are grim with nihilism? Will love save us from our fear that we are goofs who goof off? We despise a word embedded in our genomes; are we not obliged to be DRUNK? Will love save us from our fear that we are horrors too gross for words? Even as we dream we express resentment. We are tiny bees of gold, bred for the anomie of poetic labour: a never-ending message among the random shards.

The most radical flower can be smashed, all poets CRUSHED INTO poetry, the end of the world to be composed of one letter. Let us imagine a future for each atom: its reader collapses into writing itself; a reality collapses into itself; spelunkers find a way through these excerpted sentences; scribes write messages upon our tombs. Is the author an actual person who is a cadaver? Life has taught itself to write, using only writings.

These works aspire to explore the limits of their authors. What if the most radical life is a text? Diversified catastrophes crowded onto a single page? Countless details, pointless detours? You dream about a random complex of combinations ready to collapse: life is a text the shredders shred, a papyrus cadaver that can unscroll to the edge of the universe while disrupting it. Ripples that lap at the shore rewrite the loops and whorls of fingerprints.

ACKNOWLEDGEMENTS

All of the essays in this collection are written with the permission of the writers whose textual materials have been recombined. In each essay, the title, the section headers, and the sentences in the first section are direct quotations from the writer's textual corpus. All other sentences are spliced together from diverse materials found throughout the corpus.

Thank you to Annharte, Charles Bernstein, Christian Bök, Johanna Drucker, Lyn Hejinian, Steve McCaffery, Erín Moure, Sawako Nakayasu, Lisa Robertson, and Fred Wah for allowing me to write with your text.

Thank you to Erín Moure for working as an editor on this project.

Thank you to all of the publications who have shown an interest in this project: *Minor Literature[s]*, *English Studies in Canada*, *Canadian Literature*, *Berfrois*, *Polish Journal for American Studies*, *Notre Dame Review*, *Revista 404*, *Art + Research*, *The Town Crier*, *3:AM Magazine*, and *Belfield Literary Review*.

Thank you to the Alberta Foundation for the Arts and Access Copyright for helping to fund this project.

Thank you to Mark Amerika, Neil Badmington, Gregory Betts, Sigrid Hackenberg, Natalie Helberg, Michael James, Heather Jessup, Alice Major, Ana Cecilia Medina, Małgorzata Myk, Mike O'Driscoll, Julia Polyck-O'Neill, Shazia Hafiz Ramji, and Fernando Sdrigotti for helping me to share this work.

My deepest respect and gratitude to Rebecca Fredrickson.

TEXTS RECOMBINED

Annharte: *Being on the Moon* (Polestar Books, 1990), *Exercises in Lip Pointing* (New Star Books, 2003), *AKA Inendagosekwe* (edited by Reg Johanson, CUE, 2012), *Indigena Awry* (New Star Books, 2012), and interviews.

Charles Bernstein: *Shade* (Sun & Moon Press, 1978), *Senses of Responsibility* (Tuumba Press, 1979), *Poetic Justice* (Pod Books, 1979), *Controlling Interests* (Roof Books, 1980), *The Sophist* (Salt Publishing, 1987), *Rough Trades* (Sun & Moon Press, 1991), *Islets/Irritations* (Roof Books, 1992), *A Poetics* (Harvard UP, 1992), *Dark City* (Sun & Moon Press, 1994), *Close Listening: Poetry and the Performed Word* (Oxford UP, 1998), *My Way: Speeches and Poems* (U of Chicago P, 1999), *Shadowtime* (Green Integer, 2005), *Girly Man* (U of Chicago P, 2006), *Attack of the Difficult Poems* (U of Chicago P, 2011), and *Pitch of Poetry* (U of Chicago P, 2016).

Christian Bök: *Crystallography* (Coach House Books, 1994), *Eunoia* (Coach House Books, 2001), *'Pataphysics: The Poetics of an Imaginary Science* (Northwestern UP, 2001), and *The Xenotext (Book 1)* (Coach House Books, 2015).

Johanna Drucker: *From A to Z* (Chased Press, 1977), *Against Fiction: Organized Affinities* (Granary Books, 1983), *The Visible Word: Experimental Typography and Modern Art* (U of Chicago P, 1996), *SpecLab: Digital Aesthetics and Speculative Computing* (U of Chicago P, 2008), *What Is?* (Cuneiform Press, 2013), and *Graphesis: Visual Forms of Knowledge Production* (Harvard UP, 2014).

Lyn Hejinian: *Writing is an Aid to Memory* (Sun & Moon Press, 1978), *My Life* (Green Integer, 1980), *Oxota* (Wesleyan UP, 1991), *The Cell* (Sun & Moon Press, 1992), *The Cold of Poetry* (Sun & Moon Press, 1994), *The Language of Inquiry* (U of California P, 2000), *A Border Comedy* (Granary Books, 2001), *Slowly* (Tummba Press, 2002), *The Fatalist* (Omnidawn Publishing, 2003), *My Life in the Nineties* (Wesleyan UP, 2003), *Saga/Circus* (Omnidawn Publishing, 2008), *Book of a Thousand*

Eyes (Omnidawn Publishing, 2012), and *The Unfollowing* (Omnidawn Publishing, 2016).

Steve McCaffery: *Carnival* (Coach House Press, 1973), *Dr. Sadhu's Muffins* (Press Porcepic, 1974), *Ow's Waif* (Coach House Press, 1975), *Knowledge Never Knew* (Véhicule Press, 1983), *Panopticon* (blewointmentpress, 1984), *North of Intention: Critical Writings 1973–1986* (Roof Books, 1986), *Evoba* (Coach House Books, 1987), *The Black Debt* (Nightwood Editions, 1989), *Theory of Sediment* (Talonbooks, 1991), *Rational Geomancy: The Kids of the Book-Machine: The Collected Research Reports of the Toronto Research Group 1973–1982* (with bpNichol, Talonbooks, 1992), *Seven Pages Missing* (Coach House Books, 2000), *Prior to Meaning: The Protosemantic and Poetics* (Northwestern UP, 2001), and *The Darkness of the Present: Poetics, Anachronism, and the Anomaly* (U of Alabama P, 2012).

Erín Moure: *Empire, York Street* (House of Anansi Press, 1979), *The Whisky Vigil* (Harbour Press, 1981), *Wanted Alive* (House of Anansi Press, 1983), *Domestic Fuel* (House of Anansi Press, 1985), *Furious* (House of Anansi Press, 1988), *WSW* (Véhicule Press, 1989), *Sheepish Beauty, Civilian Love* (Véhicule Press, 1992), *Two Women Talking: Correspondence 1985–1987* (edited by Susan McMaster, Feminist Caucus of the League of Canadian Poets, 1993), *Search Procedures* (House of Anansi Press, 1996), *A Frame of the Book* (House of Anansi Press, 1999), *Pillage Laud* (Moveable Type, 1999), *O Cidadán* (House of Anansi Press, 2002), *Little Theatres* (House of Anansi Press, 2005), *O Cadoiro* (House of Anansi Press, 2007), *My Beloved Wager* (House of Anansi Press, 2009), *O Resplandor* (House of Anansi Press, 2010), *The Unmemntioable* (House of Anansi Press, 2012), *Secession/Insecession* (with Chus Pato, Book*hug Press, 2014), and *Kapusta* (House of Anansi Press, 2015).

Sawako Nakayasu: *So we have been given time or* (Wave Books, 2004), *Nothing fictional but the accuracy or arrangement (she* (Quale Press, 2005), *Hurry Home Honey* (Burning Deck, 2009), *Texture Notes* (Letter Machine Editions, 2010), *Mouth: Eats Color—Sagawa Chika Translations, Anti-Translations, & Originals* (Factorial Press, 2011), *The Ants* (Les Figures Press, 2014), and interviews.

Lisa Robertson: *The Apothecary* (Book*hug, 1991), *XEclogue* (New Star Books, 1993), *The Weather* (New Star Books, 2001), *Occasional Work and Seven Walks from the Office for Soft Architecture* (Coach House Books, 2003), *The Men: A Lyric Book* (Book*hug, 2006), *Lisa Robertson's Magenta Soul Whip* (Coach House Books, 2009), *R's Boat* (U of California P, 2010), *Nilling: Prose* (Book*hug, 2012), *Cinema of the Present* (Coach House Books, 2014), and *3 Summers* (Coach House Books, 2016).

Fred Wah: *Lardeau* (Island Press, 1965), *Mountain* (Audit/East-West, 1967), *Among* (Coach House Press, 1972), *Tree* (Vancouver Community Press, 1972), *Earth* (Canton, 1974), *Pictograms from the Interior of B.C.* (Talonbooks, 1975), *Owner's Manual* (Island Writing Series, 1981), *Breathin' My Name with a Sigh* (Talonbooks, 1981), *Waiting for Saskatchewan* (Turnstone Press, 1985), *Music at the Heart of Thinking* (Red Deer College Press, 1987), *So Far* (Talonbooks, 1991), *Alley Alley Home Free* (Red Deer College Press, 1992), *Diamond Grill* (NeWest Press, 1996), *Faking It: Poetics and Hybridity: Critical Writing 1984–1999* (NeWest Press, 2000), *Isadora Blue* (La Mano Izquierda Impresora, 2005), *is a door* (Talonbooks, 2009), and *Permissions: Tish Poetics 1963 Thereafter* (Ronsdale Press, 2014).

Photo Credit: Rebecca Fredrickson

Joel Katelnikoff holds a PhD in literary theory from the University of Alberta. He began working on *Recombinant Theory* in 2015. He has presented on his work at academic conferences and poetry festivals in Edmonton, Calgary, Victoria, Vancouver, Toronto, Philadelphia, Washington, Ireland, Wales, Sweden, Poland, and Slovenia.

BRAVE & BRILLIANT SERIES

SERIES EDITOR: Aritha van Herk, Professor, English, University of Calgary
ISSN 2371-7238 (PRINT) ISSN 2371-7246 (ONLINE)

No. 1 · *The Book of Sensations* | Sheri-D Wilson
No. 2 · *Throwing the Diamond Hitch* | Emily Ursuliak
No. 3 · *Fail Safe* | Nikki Sheppy
No. 4 · *Quarry* | Tanis Franco
No. 5 · *Visible Cities* | Kathleen Wall and Veronica Geminder
No. 6 · *The Comedian* | Clem Martini
No. 7 · *The High Line Scavenger Hunt* | Lucas Crawford
No. 8 · *Exhibit* | Paul Zits
No. 9 · *Pugg's Portmanteau* | D. M. Bryan
No. 10 · *Dendrite Balconies* | Sean Braune
No. 11 · *The Red Chesterfield* | Wayne Arthurson
No. 12 · *Air Salt* | Ian Kinney
No. 13 · *Legislating Love* | Play by Natalie Meisner, with Director's Notes by Jason Mehmel, and Essays by Kevin Allen and Tereasa Maillie
No. 14 · *The Manhattan Project* | Ken Hunt
No. 15 · *Long Division* | Gil McElroy
No. 16 · *Disappearing in Reverse* | Allie McFarland
No. 17 · *Phillis* | Alison Clarke
No. 18 · *DR SAD* | David Bateman
No. 19 · *Unlocking* | Amy LeBlanc
No. 20 · *Spectral Living* | Andrea King
No. 21 · *Happy Sands* | Barb Howard
No. 22 · *In Singing, He Composed a Song* | Jeremy Stewart
No. 23 · *I Wish I Could be Peter Falk* | Paul Zits
No. 24 · *A Kid Called Chatter* | Chris Kelly
No. 25 · *the book of smaller* | rob mclennan
No. 26 · *An Orchid Astronomy* | Tasnuva Hayden
No. 27 · *Not the Apocalypse I Was Hoping For* | Leslie Greentree
No. 28 · *Refugia* | Patrick Horner
No. 29 · *Five Stalks of Grain* | Adrian Lysenko, Illustrated by Ivanka Theodosia Galadza
No. 30 · *body works* | dennis cooley
No. 31 · *East Grand Lake* | Tim Ryan
No. 32 · *Muster Points* | Lucas Crawford
No. 33 · *Flicker* | Lori Hahnel
No. 34 · *Flight Risk* | A Play by Meg Braem, with Essays by William John Pratt and by David B. Hogan and Philip D. St. John, and Director's Notes by Samantha MacDonald
No. 35 · *The Signs of No* | Judith Pond
No. 36 · *Limited Verse* | David Martin
No. 37 · *We Are Already Ghosts* | Kit Dobson
No. 38 · *Invisible Lives* | Cristalle Smith
No. 39 · *Recombinant Theory* | Joel Katelnikoff

Printed by Imprimerie Gauvin
Gatineau, Québec